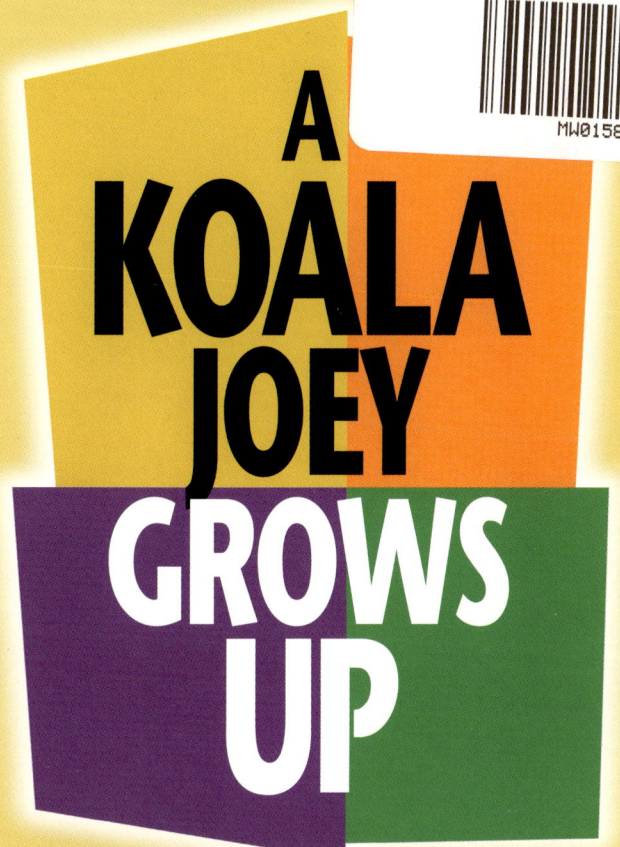

A KOALA JOEY GROWS UP

by Joan Hewett
photographs by Richard Hewett

CAROLRHODA BOOKS, INC./MINNEAPOLIS

Mel Sees Her World

Koalas live in Australia.
Most live in forests of eucalyptus trees.
This mother koala lives in a wild animal park.

She has a newborn joey in her pouch.
The joey is her baby.
The joey's name is Mel.

Mel is tiny and pink.
She stays hidden in her mother's pouch.
She drinks her mother's milk.
She grows.
She begins to look like a koala.

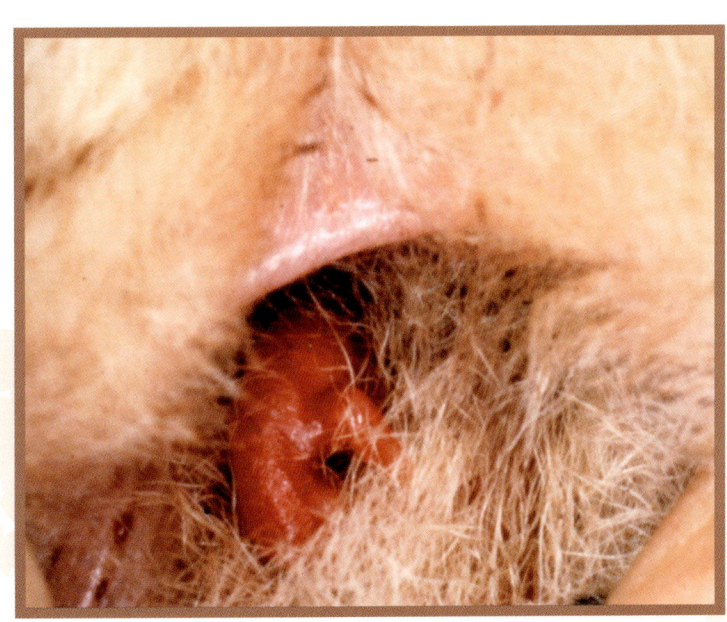

Mel is 7 months old.
The pouch is becoming too small.
Mel pushes her head out.

She takes her first peek at the world.

The koala joey is timid.
She pulls her head back inside the pouch.
She drinks her mother's milk.
She sleeps.
From time to time, she pokes her head out.

A few days later,
Mel wiggles out.
There are
strange sights.
There are
strange sounds.
Mel clings
to her mother.
She feels safe.

Mel's mother climbs a tree.
Mel rides on her belly.
Her claws grip her mother's fur.

Koalas have sharp claws.
They grip branches with their claws.

Mel needs a lot of sleep.
Even adult koalas sleep most of the time.

A nook in a tree makes a lovely bed.
Mel holds tight to her mother's fur.
Her mother holds tight to the tree.
The koalas are sound asleep.

RIDING PIGGYBACK

Mel is 8 months old.
She rides piggyback.
From her new perch,
she watches her mother climb.

Mel's mother chews a leaf.
Then she feeds
the chewed leaf to Mel.
Sometimes Mel still drinks
her mother's milk.

Mel is used to being outside. Now she will meet the people who work at the park.

Mel does not want to be held.

She does not feel safe without her mother.
How will the park workers weigh her?

They put both mother and joey on the scale.
The two animals weigh 19 pounds.
The workers know Mel's mother weighs 15 pounds.
So Mel must weigh 4 pounds.

Back outside, Mel's nose tingles.
The smell of eucalyptus fills the air.

The juiciest leaves are high up.
Mel's mother climbs into the treetops.
The koalas enjoy a tasty feast.

LEARNING TO CLIMB

Mel is 9 months old.
She rides on her mother's back.
But she'd like to be able to go
where she wants.
If only she could climb!

Mel spreads her toes.
She grips the tree trunk
with her claws.
She climbs.

Mel is 10 months old.
She climbs with ease.
She eats so many leaves
that she no longer drinks her mother's milk.

Even so, Mel stays
near her mother.
Sometimes
she takes a ride
on her mother's back.

It's time for Mel to leave her mother.
The park workers make sure Mel is healthy.

Her heartbeat is strong.
Her ears are clean.
She is a healthy young koala.

Mel enjoys her new outdoor area.
She has a favorite climbing tree.
There's a branch that's just right
for sleeping.

The gentle koala
is almost 1 year old.
She is almost
full grown.
She is ready
to be on her own.

Birth — Mel lives in her mother's pouch.

7 months old — Mel comes out of her mother's pouch.

More about Koalas

Koalas carry their babies in pouches. Animals that have pouches are called marsupials.

Koalas live in Australia. Long ago, there were large forests along Australia's eastern coast. The forests were thick with eucalyptus trees. Koalas lived in the tall trees. They ate eucalyptus leaves and bark.

The native Australians gave these animals their name. *Koala* means "no drink." The animals seldom drink water. They get their water from eucalyptus leaves.

When the sun goes down, koalas become active. It is time for them to eat. Koalas can climb up the tallest trees. They also walk on all fours with great speed. Still, these gentle animals spend more time asleep than awake.

Koalas need to eat eucalyptus leaves to stay healthy. But more and more people live in Australia. People are cutting down the great eucalyptus forests to make way for towns and farms. Once there were several million koalas. There are probably fewer than 1 million left.

People work to save and restore the remaining forests. They want the koalas to survive. You can learn more about their work. Go to the Australian Koala Foundation website at <www.savethekoala.com>.

More about Wild Animal Parks

Mel and her mother live in the Lone Pine Koala Sanctuary in Brisbane, Australia. This large park is home to 136 koalas. People who work at the park drive to nearby eucalyptus groves. They bring back truckloads of green branches, so the koalas have plenty to eat.

INDEX

climbing, 10–11, 14, 21, 23–24, 28

drinking milk, 5, 8, 15, 24

eating leaves, 15, 21, 24

mother, 3–5, 8–10, 13–15, 18–19, 21–22, 25–26

mother's pouch, 4–6, 8

park workers, 16–19, 26

riding piggyback, 14, 22, 25

sleeping, 12–13, 28–29

For our grandsons, Orson Ridgely, Jesse Angelo, and Nathan Morris

Text copyright © 2004 by Joan Hewett
Photographs copyright © 2004 by Richard R. Hewett

Photograph on page 5 used with permission of Wendy Blanshard/Australian Koala Foundation—www.savethekoala.com

All rights reserved. International copyright secured. No part of this book may be reproduced, stored in a retrieval system, or transmitted in any form or by any means—electronic, mechanical, photocopying, recording, or otherwise—without the prior written permission of Carolrhoda Books, Inc., except for brief quotations in an acknowledged review.

This book is available in two editions:
Library binding by Carolrhoda Books, Inc., a division of Lerner Publishing Group
Soft cover by First Avenue Editions, an imprint of Lerner Publishing Group
241 First Avenue North
Minneapolis, MN 55401 U.S.A.

Website address: www.lernerbooks.com

Library of Congress Cataloging-in-Publication Data

Hewett, Joan.
    A koala joey grows up / by Joan Hewett ; photographs by Richard Hewett.
       p.   cm. — (Baby animals)
    Summary: Describes the development of Mel, a koala living in a nature park, from birth to age eleven months.
      ISBN: 1–57505–198–2 (lib. bdg. : alk. paper)
      ISBN: 1–57505–631–3 (pbk. : alk. paper)
    1. Koala—Infancy—Juvenile literature. [1. Koala. 2. Animals—Infancy.] I. Hewett, Richard, ill. II. Title. III. Series.
QL737.M384H49 2004
599.2'5139—dc22
2003011753

Manufactured in the United States of America
1 2 3 4 5 6 – DP – 09 08 07 06 05 04